Junior High Bible Study Series

Choosing Wisely

Group
Loveland, Colorado

Group's R.E.A.L. Guarantee to you:

This Group resource incorporates our R.E.A.L. approach to ministry—one that encourages long-term retention and life transformation. It's ministry that's:

Relational
Because learner-to-learner interaction enhances learning and builds Christian friendships.

Experiential
Because what learners experience through discussion and action sticks with them up to 9 times longer than what they simply hear or read.

Applicable
Because the aim of Christian education is to equip learners to be both hearers and doers of God's Word.

Learner-based
Because learners understand and retain more when the learning process takes into consideration how they learn best.

Choosing Wisely

Junior High Bible Study Series

Copyright © 2004 Group Publishing, Inc.

Visit our Web site: **www.group.com**

Credits
Contributing Authors: Trudy Hewitt, Mikal Keefer, Karl Leuthauser, and Amy Simpson
Editors: Tammy L. Bicket and Dawn M. Brandon
Acquisitions Editor: Kelli B. Trujillo
Creative Development Editor: Amy Simpson
Chief Creative Officer: Joani Schultz
Copy Editor: Marilyn Welsh
Art Director: Jane Parenteau
Print Production Artist: Joyce Douglas
Illustrator: Matt Wood
Cover Art Director/Designer: Jeff A. Storm
Cover Photographer: Daniel Treat
Production Manager: DeAnne Lear

ISBN 0-7644-2486-6
10 9 8 7 6 5 4 3 2   13 12 11 10 09 08 07 06 05

Printed in the United States of America.

Table of Contents

Choosing Wisely

Decisions, decisions...life is full of choices to make. What to wear, where to go, what to eat for lunch, what car to drive, what college to attend, or what career to pursue. But there are even more important choices that we make every day, and often they affect us in ways we may not realize. But they do affect us, especially in our spiritual lives.

Making good choices can be tough even for adults, but you're never too young to learn to choose wisely. In fact, the choices your junior highers make today could affect their lives not just today but for years to come. *Choosing Wisely* helps you guide your students into making wise choices that will please God and give them a head start on successful, fulfilling, God-honoring lives.

The first study helps students understand that when God is in their hearts, their values should reflect his. Junior highers will learn that God's values are different from the world's. While the world places a premium on shallow outward appearances, God sees and values true beauty of the heart. This study will help students resolve to choose God's values.

In the second study, students will learn the importance of choosing to focus their thoughts on good things. The world bombards teenagers with negative, destructive, and evil messages. These unholy messages blast us brazenly or subtly slip past the defenses of our hearts through the entertainment we embrace. This study gives teenagers guidance in evaluating and choosing the messages and images they will allow into their minds.

In the third study, junior highers will learn that God wants them to choose to love their enemies. Our society tends to portray love as something you can't control. We "fall in love." Either we love someone or we don't. But Jesus shows us a better way. Although loving those who have hurt us isn't natural, Jesus has called his followers to choose to demonstrate supernatural, Christlike love to everyone.

In the fourth study, students will learn that God doesn't leave us on our own to make good choices. We don't have to follow our own instincts or obey our sinful impulses. The Holy Spirit helps teenagers make good choices. All they have to do is ask for his help and guidance.

Choosing Wisely is a powerful study with the potential to transform your students' lives right now and for the future. You'll be glad you chose it!

Choosing Wisely helps you guide your students into making wise choices that will please God and give them a head start on successful, fulfilling, God-honoring lives.

junior high bible study series
About Faith 4 Life™

Use Faith 4 Life studies to show your teenagers how the Bible is relevant to their lives. Help them see that God can invade every area of their lives and change them in ways they can only imagine. Encourage your students to go deeper into faith—faith that will sustain them for life! Faith 4 Life forever!

Faith 4 Life™: Junior High Bible Study Series helps young teenagers take a Bible-based approach to faith and life issues. Each book in the series contains these important elements:

■ **Life application of Bible truth**—Faith 4 Life studies help teenagers understand what the Bible says and then apply that truth to their lives.

■ **A relevant topic**—Each Faith 4 Life book focuses on one main topic, with four studies to give your students a thorough understanding of how the Bible relates to that topic. These topics were chosen by youth leaders as the ones most relevant for junior high students.

■ **One point**—Each study makes one point, centering on that one theme to make sure students really understand the important truth it conveys. This point is stated upfront and throughout the study.

■ **Simplicity**—The studies are easy to use. Each contains a "Before the Study" box that outlines any advance preparation required. Each study also contains a "Study at a Glance" chart so that you can quickly and easily see what supplies you'll need and what each study will involve.

■ **Action and interaction**—Each study relies on experiential learning to help students learn what God's Word has to say. Teenagers discuss and debrief their experiences in large groups, small groups, and individual reflection.

■ **Reproducible handouts**—Faith 4 Life books include reproducible handouts for students. No need for student books!

■ **Tips, tips, and more tips**—Faith 4 Life studies are full of "FYI" tips for the teacher, providing extra ideas, insights into young people, and hints for making the studies go smoothly.

■ **Flexibility**—Faith 4 Life studies include optional activities and bonus activities. Use a study as it's written, or use these options to create the study that works best for your group.

■ **Follow-up ideas**—At the end of each book, you'll find a section called "Changed 4 Life." This section provides ideas for following up with your students to make sure the Bible truths stick with them.

Choosing God's Values

With so many influences coming from so many sources, we need to be committed to helping junior highers understand God's desires for their lives. This study will show them what God values in a Christian's life.

God sent Samuel to Bethlehem to select a king to replace Saul. Visiting the home of Jesse, Samuel found seven tall, strong, and handsome sons who looked like great choices for a leader. He was convinced that God would choose one of these men. But instead God chose David, the eighth and youngest son, who was merely a shepherd.

David's heart was more important to God than the older brothers' looks or outward qualifications. Acts 13:22 records God's reason for choosing David: "I have found David son of Jesse a man after my own heart; he will do everything I want him to do." David's heart was attuned to God. He reflected the values that are important to God.

Through this story, God reminds teenagers, as he reminded Samuel, that while the world is impressed by outward appearances, God looks at hearts. Junior highers live in a world where values are upside down. Rebellion against authority is admired. Those who abuse their bodies with sex, drugs, and alcohol are considered popular—maybe even celebrities. Being smart, rich, fashionable, and thin can seem like the most important values to pursue for happiness and fulfillment. But God blows those shallow values out of the water. Today, help your students learn what God truly values and commit to choosing to reflect those values in their own lives.

CHRIST REFLECTION

The Study at a Glance

Warm-Up (15-20 minutes)

Auction, Auction!
What students will do: Participate in an auction to purchase "goods."

Needs: ❑ newsprint
❑ marker
❑ various "auctionable" items
❑ play money
❑ bag

Bonus Activity (5-10 minutes)
What students will do: Use clay to create something they value.

❑ modeling clay

Bible Connection (20-25 minutes)

Bag-Full of Me
What students will do: Decorate masks that reflect how others see them, then show a side of themselves that others don't see.

Needs: ❑ paper grocery bags
❑ markers
❑ Bible

Life Application (10-15 minutes)

Reflect on This
What students will do: See specific ways their values should reflect God, evaluate their own lives, and spend time in prayer seeking to reflect God's values.

Needs: ❑ mirror
❑ "Reflecting God's Values" handouts (pp. 13-14)

The Point

▶ When God is in our hearts, our lives should reflect his values.

Scripture Source

1 Samuel 16:1-13
God chooses a king for Israel.

VALUES

CHRIST REFLECTION

For the "Auction, Auction!" activity, gather a variety of items for an auction—candy, coupons, pencils, soft drinks, books, CDs, never-claimed items from lost-and-found, and so on. Arrange these on a table, and put a large amount of play money of various denominations in a bag (or write one, five, ten, twenty, fifty, and one hundred on pieces of paper instead).

For the "Reflect on This" activity, cut apart sections of the "Reflecting God's Values" handout (pp. 13-14). You may wish to make copies for your teenagers to take home at the end of the session so they will be reminded of God's values and the importance of reflecting him in their hearts.

Auction, Auction!

(15 to 20 minutes)

Write the word *Values* at the top of a sheet of newsprint.

SAY:

■ Let's take a minute to brainstorm some definitions of this word.

Encourage teenagers to suggest possible meanings of the word *values*. Students might offer answers like priorities, honesty, or code of conduct. Write their ideas on the newsprint. Then

ASK:

■ Was it easy for you to define this word? Why or why not?

SAY:

■ Defining values may be easy or difficult, but applying them to our lives and the choices we make is something we all struggle with. Today we're going to look at the best values one can have: God's values.

Put a large amount of play money of various values (or slips of paper with numbers written on them) in a bag and have students reach inside and take two bills. Then indicate the variety of items you arranged before class and

SAY:

■ We're going to have an auction. You can buy something from

If teenagers have a hard time defining *values*, share some of these definitions:

■ Ideas or beliefs that are very important to someone.

■ Characteristics or ideals that reflect what someone loves or highly esteems.

■ Principles or standards that govern behavior.

this group of items with the "money" you have, or you can form a pool with others to buy something to share.

Begin the bidding, keeping a quick pace. After all the items have been purchased,

ASK:

■ How did you feel during the auction? Explain.
■ How did our auction reflect our values?

SAY:

The Point ▶ ■ You can tell what people value by what they spend their money on and what they spend their time doing. <u>When God is in our hearts, our lives should reflect his values.</u> But what does God value? Let's look at what the Bible says.

You may wish to bring pictures of items of greater worldly value and encourage teenagers to bid on them: cars, jewelry, clothing, shoes, electronics, and so on. You can find appropriate pictures in catalogs, magazines, and sales fliers. Be sure to include items that are valuable by God's standards as well as those that are valuable by the world's standards. You might even write "self-respect," "the opportunity to help a stranger," "sacrifice," and other things God would value on pieces of paper or small boxes and make them items for auction. You'll need higher values of play money for these items. Or consider allowing students to write one "blank check" for the item they value most.

Bonus Activity

(5 to 10 minutes)

If you have time, try this extra activity to begin your Bible study.

Give students each a hunk of clay, and tell them they have two minutes to mold it into something they value greatly, such as a car, a boyfriend or girlfriend, clothes or money. When finished, have teenagers each find a partner and share how having this value has affected their actions. For example, if they value clothes, they may work in order to have more money for their wardrobes.

When everyone has shared,

ASK:

■ What are ways your values affect your actions?
■ How does having the value you expressed make you feel?
■ Why do you think valuing something affects our choices and behavior?

The Point ▶ ■ Everybody values something. <u>When God is in our hearts, our lives should reflect his values.</u> Today we're going to talk about the things God values and why these are the best things we can value.

Bag-Full of Me

(20 to 25 minutes)

Give each student a large, paper grocery bag, and provide markers to be shared by all.

SAY:

■ Take your bag and determine where holes for eyes should be. Tear these out. Then write words or draw pictures on the outside of your bag, expressing characteristics others see when they look at you. For example, you might draw a smile or write the word *happy*. These words or drawings don't have to represent how you feel about yourself, but rather how you think others see you. On the inside of the bag, draw or write things representing what you feel is important about yourself that others may not know.

When students are finished, have them put their bags over their heads and form groups of no more than four. In their groups, have students look at the outside of one another's bags and determine what the words or drawings represent.

Read 1 Samuel 16:1-13 aloud, and have groups summarize the story in their own words. When each group has shared,

ASK:

■ From these verses, what do you think God values?

■ How do you feel when people judge you based on the things on the outside of your bag?

■ How are the things that seem important to others different from the things God values?

SAY:

■ As you all wear your bags, you look a lot alike. It's what's on the inside that makes each of you very special. It's nice to know that God values what's on the inside of us rather than on the outside. But let's make sure that what's on the inside is pleasing to him. We want to be our best on the inside too.

Have students remain in their groups and take off their paper bags. Have markers available.

SAY:

■ Turn your bags inside out and look at the words or pictures on your bag. See if any of them represent values not pleasing to God or even just things you'd like to change. Draw a line through any of these things, and pray as a group for God to bring about change in these areas.

When students have prayed, ask them to put their bags back on their heads, inside out.

SAY:

■ While wearing your bags with your "real" side showing, write on the bags of your group members the things you think God values in their lives. For example, you might write that God values their commitment to the youth group or their kindness to others.

When everyone has done this, gather the group together and let teenagers remove their bags again.

SAY:

The Point ▶ ■ <u>When God is in our hearts, our lives should reflect his values.</u> We make ourselves more beautiful on the inside by choosing values that please and reflect God. No matter what others see on the outside, God is still looking at the part of you that matters most: the inside.

Life Application | Reflect on This

(10 to 15 minutes)

Divide the class into groups of three, and give each student one piece of the "Reflecting God's Values" handout (pp. 13-14). Have a large mirror available at the front of the room.

SAY:

The Point ▶ ■ <u>When God is in our hearts, our lives should reflect his values.</u>

But how do we know what those values are? When God is living in our hearts, he influences us and speaks to us so we often just seem to know what he values and what he doesn't. But we can't always go by our feelings, our consciences. God's Word gives us clear instruction about some values we should share with God.

Each of you has a slip of paper that has an important instruction from God's Word. It doesn't seem too clear when you look at it with natural eyes, but when you look at it in the mirror, it becomes clear. This is how it is when we try to figure out what God values through the natural lens of this world. Because of the presence of sin, the world warps things, skews God's truth, and sees things differently than God does. But as Christians, we need to learn to see things as God does, no matter how the world sees them or what it values.

Have members of different trios take turns going to the mirror, holding their messages up to it, and reading the messages out loud. Between the three group members, they must explain their messages and come up with practical examples of how Christian teenagers should act upon those values.

When everyone has taken a turn, ask students to silently and prayerfully evaluate their own lives. Ask the following questions, pausing after each to let students quietly consider their responses.

ASK:

- How does your life line up with these values?
- In what areas do you need to improve?
- How much impact is your relationship with Jesus having on what you value and how you live?
- Are your values and life choices aligned more with God's or with the world's?
- You may look like a model Christian on the outside, but what counts is what's in your heart. How pleased is God with the condition of your heart?

Encourage junior highers to spend a few minutes in individual prayer, asking God to help them line up with and reflect God's values in their life choices. Then encourage teenagers to pray briefly for the other two students in their trio. Conclude the study by leading teenagers in prayer, asking God to help them reflect God's values in their hearts.

If you have less than twelve students, give some (or all) more than one section of the "Reflecting God's Values" handout (pp. 13-14). If you have more than twelve, make several copies of each section so all teenagers can be involved in reading and applying God's values to their lives.

You may want to give every student a copy of the entire "Reflecting God's Values" handout (pp. 13-14) to take home as a reminder of the values that reflect God in their hearts. Encourage students to read them in a mirror every few days as a gauge of their progress.

REFLECTING GOD'S VALUES

GENEROSITY

"God loves a cheerful giver." (2 Corinthians 9:7).

- -

JUSTICE AND MERCY

"He has showed you, O man, what is good. And what does the Lord require of you? To act justly and to love mercy and to walk humbly with your God." (Micah 6:8).

- -

CHRISTLIKE LOVE

"Love is patient, love is kind. It does not envy, it does not boast, it is not proud. It is not rude, it is not self-seeking, it is not easily angered, it keeps no record of wrongs. Love does not delight in evil but rejoices with the truth. It always protects, always trusts, always hopes, always perseveres." (1 Corinthians 13:4-7).

- -

CHARITY AND PURITY

"Religion that God our Father accepts as pure and faultless is this: to look after orphans and widows in their distress and to keep oneself from being polluted by the world." (James 1:27).

- -

HEAVENLY RICHES

"Do not store up for yourselves treasures on earth, where moth and rust destroy, and where thieves break in and steal. But store up for yourselves treasures in heaven, where moth and rust do not destroy, and where thieves do not break in and steal. For where your treasure is, there your heart will be also." (Matthew 6:19-21).

- -

SERVICE

"Whoever wants to be first must be slave of all." (Mark 10:44).

- -

NOT OF THIS WORLD

"Do not love the world or anything in the world. If anyone loves the world, the love of the Father is not in him" (1 John 2:15).

LOVING OTHERS

"We love because he first loved us. If anyone says, 'I love God,' yet hates his brother, he is a liar. For anyone who does not love his brother, whom he has seen, cannot love God, whom he has not seen. And he has given us this command: Whoever loves God must also love his brother." (1 John 4:19-21).

KINDNESS TO THE NEEDY

"He who is kind to the poor lends to the Lord, and he will reward him for what he has done" (Proverbs 19:17).

NO FAVORITISM

"If you really keep the royal law found in Scripture, 'Love your neighbor as yourself,' you are doing right. But if you show favoritism, you sin and are convicted by the law as lawbreakers" (James 2:8-9).

THE WHOLE TRUTH

" 'These are the things you are to do: Speak the truth to each other, and render true and sound judgment in your courts; do not plot evil against your neighbor, and do not love to swear falsely. I hate all this,' declares the Lord." (Zechariah 8:16-17).

KEEPING IT CLEAN

"The things that come out of the mouth come from the heart, and these make a man 'unclean.' For out of the heart come evil thoughts, murder, adultery, sexual immorality, theft, false testimony, slander. These are what make a man 'unclean'; but eating with unwashed hands does not make him 'unclean.' " (Matthew 15:18-20).

Good Thinking

GUARDING

mind

"It doesn't affect me," teenagers often rationalize about violence in their video games and movies, foul language on television or in music, and immoral lifestyles glamorized in every type of "entertainment." But everything we allow inside us does affect us. While it's easy to forget the date Columbus discovered America or the three branches of government, graphic images in movies and subtle worldviews expressed in popular television and songs get stuck in our heads like a tune you can't shake. It *does* matter what we allow in our minds, even our entertainment. Maybe especially our entertainment. For its philosophies and evil sneak in the back door while we relax and let our guard down in order to be entertained.

Evil is everywhere, not only in movies, but in video games, music, the Internet, books, and comic books. Many junior high students may not realize that participating in these activities can be harmful. In fact, they may feel some resistance to the very idea that it's something they shouldn't get involved with. Yet even those students have probably also experienced a "prick" in their consciences while consuming trashy entertainment.

God warns us to be careful of what we see, hear, and think about. He instructs us to choose to fill our minds with things that are good, positive, lovely, and true. This study will help teenagers learn how to recognize damaging, negative influences in today's entertainment and what potential damage or dangers are inherent in allowing such images and thoughts into our minds. Teenagers will be given the opportunity to decide where they need to draw the line—even when it's a hard decision.

The Point

▶ We should honor God in our entertainment choices.

Scripture Source

Ephesians 6:12
Paul explains that we are in a spiritual struggle.

Philippians 4:8
Paul reminds us to dwell on pure and holy things.

Colossians 3:5-6
Paul tells us to avoid being controlled by immoral or indecent things.

GUARDING

mind

The Study at a Glance

Warm-Up (15-20 minutes)

Evil's Lure
What students will do: Participate in a skit demonstrating how Satan uses entertainment to involve us in evil.

Needs: ❑ "Stop Them!" handouts (pp. 24–25)
❑ paper ❑ pens
❑ props (optional)

Bible Connection (25-30 minutes)

Review: These Movies Stink!
What students will do: Recognize the importance of selecting positive entertainment and review current music, movies, television, games, and magazines according to biblical standards.

Needs: ❑ Bibles ❑ opaque plastic bags
❑ chopped onions ❑ crushed garlic cloves
❑ magazines ❑ video games
❑ comic books ❑ pens
❑ sliced lemons or oranges
❑ assorted videos and DVDs
❑ CDs with printed lyrics
❑ sticky notes (optional)
❑ current television and movie listings with synopses or reviews

Life Application (5-10 minutes)

Bad Memories
What students will do: Consider how things stay in our brains.

Needs: ❑ Bible ❑ tape
❑ white paper ❑ black construction paper
❑ copies of the handout described in the "Before the Study" box

Optional Activity (5-10 minutes)
What students will do: Use the flash of a camera and the resulting picture to show how things stay in our brains.

Needs: ❑ camera with flash

Before the Study

For the "Evil's Lure" activity, make a copy of the skit "Stop Them!" (pp. 24-25) for every student or every pair. Gather simple props (such as CDs, videos, video games, paper tickets, books or magazines), if you choose to use them.

For the "Review: These Movies Stink!" activity, chop a fresh onion, crush fresh garlic cloves, and slice fresh lemons or oranges. Put each into a plastic bag that you can't see through (like a bag from book or clothing stores), and close them up tightly to keep the odor inside. Gather a collection of music CDs, videos and DVDs, video games, magazines, comic books, and a copy of the current television and movie listings (with synopses and/or reviews, if possible). All of them should be geared toward junior highers. Some should be Christian, some secular, and some neutral. Some should be acceptable, some questionable, and some inadvisable for Christian teenagers. (Be careful not to select anything beyond the limits of what should be viewed in a teenage classroom setting.) Be sure the CDs have lyrics printed on the liners so students can read and evaluate them.

For the "Bad Memories" activity, create a handout similar to the diagram in the margin by taping a circle of black construction paper to a white sheet of paper. Make one photocopy of the handout for each student.

If you choose to do the Optional Activity, bring a camera with a flash to class.

Warm-Up

If you have four teenagers playing the good teenagers, have only one take the movie ticket, one take the games, and one take the music. Also change the wording from "some were" to "one was."

Evil's Lure
(15 to 20 minutes)

SAY:

■ We're going to do a skit about good and evil, and I need everybody to help. I need one person to act the part of Satan. The rest of you will either be "good teenagers" or act as Satan's demons.

Have about two-thirds of your students play the good teenagers and the remaining third act as the demons. Have one student play the part of Satan. Give each student a copy of the "Stop Them!" handout (pp. 24-25).

SAY:

■ Good teenagers can stand up front and pantomime doing

good things, such as praying, singing, and reading the Bible. Teenagers who are playing demons should stand at the back of the room. The person portraying Satan will enter when I start to read. I'll read the narrator part, and you'll act out whatever I describe or what's written in your characters' lines of the skit. You'll also need to read your lines.

After everyone is in place, begin the skit on the "Stop Them!" handout (pp. 24–25). After the skit, **ASK** those who played the demons or Satan:

- How did it feel to play an evil character?
- Do you think Satan and demons really work like this? Explain.

ASK those who played the good teenagers:

- What was it like to be tempted by those playing demons?
- How were the choices you made in this skit like or unlike choices you make in real life?

ASK everyone:

- Do you think the skit gave an accurate representation of today's entertainment? Why or why not?
- How can Satan use entertainment to plant evil in our minds?
- What sorts of evil and sin are portrayed as the norm, as being OK or even glamorous and desirable in television, movies, music, video games, and other forms of entertainment today?
- How much do these things influence your life and your ideas of what's right and what's wrong?
- How do they influence your mood?
- How do they influence your outlook on life?

Form groups of three or four and give each group a sheet of paper and a pen. Ask each group to make a list of where evil is found in our society. Give groups two or three minutes for this task. Have each group share some of the examples.

ASK:

- Why do you like or dislike some of the things we've mentioned?
- Some people say they've actually felt drawn to horror, violence, and the "dark side" of music and entertainment. What appeal do you think these dark subjects have for us?
- Why would Satan want us to be involved in such things?
- Would God want us to be involved in them? Why or why not?
- Is there a difference in types of horror, violence, and dark themes in entertainment? Are some OK and some not OK? How can we know?

Consider including props for teenagers to use during this skit, such as movie tickets, pencils, paper, cards, and CDs.

Some teenagers may share opinions counter to God's Word. Don't be defensive. Your job is to share information and God's truth. Teenagers will have to make their own decisions regarding that information.

Bible Connection

Review: These Movies Stink!
(25 to 30 minutes)

Divide the class into three groups. Give each group a plastic bag that you prepared before the study.

SAY:

■ Take turns sticking one hand into the bag and feeling what's inside. Without looking inside your bag, see if you can figure out what's in it. Touch what's inside and explore it with your fingers until you think you might know what it is. Don't say anything, but give the bag to the next person in your group. See if all of you agree as to what's in the bag.

When everyone has had a turn, have groups look inside their bags and then discuss these questions.

■ How easy or difficult was it to determine what was in your bag?

■ Do you like what's in your bag? Why or why not?

■ How does what was inside your bag still impact you even now, minutes after you touched it?

■ How long do you think the smell of what you touched will last?

■ Is the way these smells get absorbed into our skin similar to how what we choose to watch, hear, and think gets absorbed into our minds and hearts? Why or why not?

■ What kind of "odor" does watching or participating in swearing, immorality, violence, or evil leave in someone's life? Explain.

■ What kinds of positive things can we put into our minds that will leave a good "fragrance"?

SAY:

■ Everything we watch, listen to, read, think about, and focus on has an impact on our lives and our spirits. Good things have a positive, uplifting, encouraging effect. Evil things have a negative, destructive, dangerous effect. It's very important that, as Christians, we feed our minds with good

things and steer clear of the bad things. <u>We need to honor</u> ◀ **The Point**
<u>God with what we put into our minds, especially when it</u>
<u>comes to entertainment.</u> Knowing how to distinguish
between what's good and what's bad is essential for Christians. So let's practice evaluating the things we choose to
allow into our minds.

Give the first group a selection of popular contemporary music CDs with words
printed on the liners. Give the second group some videos or DVDs and current television and movie listings with synopses or previews. Give the third group a
selection of video games, comic books, and/or magazines targeted to teenagers.
Be sure to include some good, some not good, and some neutral in each selection.

Have students in each group number off: one, two, one, two, and so on. Ask a
student who is a one to read Ephesians 6:12 aloud. Then

SAY:

■ Some things we could choose to watch, read, or listen to are
part of this spiritual battle for our minds and souls. Those
of you who are ones are to examine the material your group
has been given to evaluate its spiritual content. Is the spiritual content of each item God-honoring and positive? Or
does it feature the occult, witches, spells, ghosts, demons,
characters with supernatural powers, and so on?

Ask a student who is a two to read Colossians 3:5–6 aloud. Then

SAY:

■ Some things we could choose to watch, read, or listen to
expose us to sin—sexual immorality, impurity, lust, evil desires,
greed, and other indecent things. Such things plant images,
words, and thoughts in our minds. Foul language can be hard to
get out of our minds once it gets inside. Some music, movies,
and other forms of entertainment make immorality seem
acceptable or even desirable. Those of you who are twos are to
examine your group's material to evaluate its morality content.
Would watching, reading, playing, or listening to each thing you
evaluate reinforce God's standards of right and wrong, or would
it expose your mind to impure thoughts and images?

Ask someone in each group to turn to Philippians 4:8. Read it aloud, instruct-
ing students to use it as an evaluation tool when reviewing their materials.

SAY:

■ <u>We should honor God in our entertainment choices,</u> so when ◀ **The Point** you're evaluating each item, give it the Philippians 4:8 test. Is the program, song, movie, game, or magazine true? Is it noble? Is it right? Is it pure, lovely, admirable, excellent, and praiseworthy? If not, should you be exposing your mind to it?

Give groups ten minutes to evaluate and organize the material into positive and negative piles. You may want to give each group a pad of sticky notes and ask them to write a brief explanation of their decision and attach it to each item reviewed.

Ask each group to give a brief report on what it discovered about the content of the items it evaluated—and a thumbs up or thumbs down recommendation for other teenagers, indicating whether they should choose that item for entertainment.

Life Application

Bad Memories
(5 to 10 minutes)

Give each student a copy of the handout with the black circle that you prepared before the study. Have teenagers stare at the black circle for one minute. Then have teenagers look at a white wall.

ASK:

■ How many of you can see the outline of the circle on the wall?

■ What does the fact that some of you can still see it say about our memories? our brains?

■ Picture a sunset (pause), a pen (pause), a scene from a horror film (pause). Were you able to picture those items? What feelings did you have with each picture?

■ What does that say about the things we should watch or look at?

SAY:

■ God made our brains in an incredible way. We can store memories and pictures for a long time. However, sometimes when things go into our brains, they don't go away as easily as we'd like. For example, if I asked you to describe some of the scenes from a horror film, you probably could.

ASK:

■ Do you think it's bad that you can recall those scenes? Explain.

Ask for a volunteer to read Philippians 4:8 aloud while teenagers follow along in their Bibles.

ASK:

- Why do you think we're supposed to think of these types of things?
- Does this verse have any bearing on the way you think about violent, immoral, or evil entertainment? Explain.
- How would focusing on good things, like Paul is saying here, affect the things we can picture in our minds?

SAY:

- When we focus on good things, we'll help keep our minds clear of the impure or unhealthy thoughts and images God wants us to avoid. Now that's good thinking!

Have students find prayer partners and share with each other three things they will each change in the upcoming week when it comes to entertainment choices. Then have them spend a few minutes praying for each other, asking God to help them honor him in their entertainment choices. Then ask stu- ◀ **The Point** dents to spend a moment in silent prayer, personally committing to use God's filters to choose wisely what entertainment they will take in.

FYI

We find evil in many places in our society. Teenagers often don't see a problem with playing violent video games or watching sexually graphic movies or going to haunted houses. This may be a tough subject, and some of them may really struggle with it.

Teenagers, like all of us, are prone to dabble in sin. They aren't always immersed in it—but some of them get pulled in anyway. Examine the parable of the sower in Mark 4 to help teenagers understand that "playing" with things like horror can create the thorns that choke out spiritual growth.

Optional Activity

(5 to 10 minutes)

Instead of using the black circle on white paper in "Bad Memories," consider gathering your group together for a couple of pictures. Snap their pictures using a camera with a flash. Then

ASK:

- Do you still see the light of the flash?
- How about if you close your eyes? Do you see it?
- Why do we see the flash even after it's gone?
- How is that like the lingering impact of what we see in what we choose as entertainment—movies, television, video games, or other things?

SAY:

- That moment is past, but we'll always be able to remember it with the photograph once it's developed. That's how our minds work too. Long after we've seen, heard, or read something, it lives on in our memories and can pop to the surface at any time. That's why it's so important for us to choose to focus on good things.

 FYI Once you get the photograph developed, be sure to hang it up in your meeting area as a lasting memory of what the students learned during this study.

Have students find prayer partners and spend a few minutes praying for each other, asking

Point ▶ God to help them <u>honor him in their entertainment choices</u>. Then ask students to spend a moment in silent prayer, personally committing to use God's filters to choose their entertainment wisely.

Stop Them!

Narrator: Satan was mad!

Satan: *(Acts out being mad and screams.)* I'm so mad!

Narrator: Satan called his demons, and they all came running.

Demons: *(All come running toward Satan from the back of the room.)*

Satan: *(Points toward teenagers.)* I want you to go over and look at what those teenagers are doing.

Demons: *(Surround good teenagers to see what they're doing.)*

Satan: I really hate it when teenagers are doing good things!

Narrator: So Satan called his demons back over.

Demons: *(Run back to Satan.)*

Satan: We need a plan.

Demons: *(Hold hands up with a "What should we do?" look.)*

Satan: Stop them! They're doing good. Get them to do evil instead.

Narrator: The demons protested that teenagers focusing on good things weren't interested in evil.

Satan: We need a scheme.

Narrator: The demons put their heads together.

Demons: *(Pretend to bump heads.)*

Narrator: They tried to come up with a scheme.

Demons: *(Pace and scratch heads, then surround good teenagers.)*

Narrator: The demons suggested all kinds of evil a disobedient and gross stuff.

Demons: *(Mime making evil suggestions.)*

Narrator: But the good teenagers were just too bu focusing on good things to hear the evil thoughts, and they ignored the demons.

Good Teenagers: *(Ignore demons.)*

Narrator: The demons were worried. They paced an wrung their hands.

Demons: *(Wring hands and pace.)*

Narrator: Suddenly the demons figured it out, and they jumped up and down and got excited!

Demons: *(Jump up and down, run over to Satan, a mime telling him something.)*

Satan: So if we make evil seem fun, we'll get the good teenagers too? I love your idea! How ca we make evil seem fun?

Narrator: The demons put their heads together aga

Demons: *(Pretend to bump heads.)*

Narrator: The demons just weren't sure how to ma it look fun, and they began pacing and worryi again.

Demons: *(Pace, worry, and wring hands.)*

Narrator: Suddenly they figured it out!

mons: *(Jump up and down.)*

rrator: The demons ran to tell Satan they knew how to get the teenagers to quit focusing on good things.

mons: *(Run over to Satan and mime telling him their idea.)*

tan: So we could make evil look like entertainment? I really love this idea! Go for it!

rrator: The demons got busy thinking up movies and games and books and songs.

mons: *(Write things, then throw papers in the air before running over to the good teenagers.)*

rrator: The demons surrounded the good teenagers and handed out movie tickets.

mons: *(Hand out tickets.)*

rrator: Some of the teenagers were interested, took the tickets, and left the group to see the movies.

od Teenagers: *(One or two take the tickets and leave.)*

rrator: They brought evil games.

mons: *(Pass out games or cards.)*

Narrator: Some more teenagers left because they wanted to play the games.

Good Teenagers: *(One or two good teenagers show interest in the games, take them, and leave.)*

Narrator: They gave out tapes, CDs, books, and magazines.

Demons: *(Give out tapes, CDs, books, and magazines.)*

Narrator: A lot of teenagers liked those, and they left too.

Good Teenagers: *(One or two quit what they're doing, look at the items, take some, and leave.)*

Narrator: There were only a few teenagers left doing good things.

Good Teenagers: *(Look at those who left.)*

Narrator: The demons were satisfied.

Demons: *(Give high fives.)*

Narrator: And Satan was happy.

Satan: *(Acts happy.)* I'm happy, happy, happy!

Narrator: The end.

OK2COPY

Choosing to Love

ENEMIES

love

Enemies. Your teenagers are old enough to have them. They may be as fleeting as a classmate who taunts a girl about a "bad hair day" or as permanent as an abusive parent. There's nothing rare about having enemies, but there can be something extraordinary about how your teenagers deal with their enemies.

Jesus told his followers to respond to enemies not with a fist but with love. It may be the least natural response, but Jesus made it clear that's what he expected. Jesus not only talked about it, he also demonstrated how to do it.

Why did Jesus insist that we give our tormentors such a break? And how do we manage to show love when our first instinct is to strike back at anyone who takes a swing at us?

This study will help teenagers explore strategies for handling enemies and discover how to respond in ways that can turn most enemies into friends. By learning how to feel and express compassion, your teenagers will not only become more heartfelt followers of Jesus, but they'll also discover that their world stretches beyond their own personal concerns. They'll discover that by choosing to love, they can impact others—and their world—in a positive way.

The Study at a Glance

Warm-Up (15-20 minutes)

Compassion Rations
What students will do: Identify stories about enemies in magazines and newspapers, and contrast most people's responses to enemies with the way Jesus wants us to respond.

Needs: ❏ Bible   ❏ newspapers
             ❏ magazines   ❏ newsprint
             ❏ marker   ❏ tape

Bible Connection (15-20 minutes)

Enemies: Ya Gotta Love 'Em
What students will do: Discuss where enemies come from and consider how group members have contributed to the supply.

Needs: ❏ Bibles   ❏ newsprint
             ❏ marker   ❏ tape

Bonus Activity (15-20 minutes)
What students will do: Play a "TV game show" and discover that there's a cost for forgiveness and compassion.

Needs: ❏ Bible   ❏ paper
             ❏ markers
             ❏ "Someone's Gotta Pay!" handout (p. 35)
             ❏ video camera and videotape
                (optional)

Life Application (15-20 minutes)

Loving and Letting Go
What students will do: Brainstorm ways to respond lovingly in real-life situations, then plan compassionate acts or words they can share.

Needs: ❏ slips of paper ❏ pens
             ❏ hat   ❏ buckets or tarp
             ❏ stones   ❏ pebbles

The Point

▶ You can choose to love everyone, even your enemies.

Scripture Source

Matthew 5:23-24
Jesus describes the priority that God places on healing damaged relationships and the Christian's responsibility for taking the first step.

Matthew 5:43-48
Jesus describes one way Christians should be different from others: We should love our enemies.

Luke 6:27-36
Jesus speaks some shocking words about a new way to treat enemies.

ENEMIES

love

For the "Compassion Rations" activity, stack old newspapers and magazines in the middle of the room. Copy these two lists of discussion questions for the "Compassion Rations" activity onto a piece of newsprint and tape them to a wall:

(First list)

- Who are the enemies in your story?
- Why are the enemies at odds?
- What would it take for the enemies to become friends?

(Second list)

- If you were one of the enemies in your story, could you choose to love as Jesus commands? Why or why not?
- If the enemies in your story were loving to each other, how would they behave?
- Describe a time when you've been compassionate toward someone who treated you poorly. Was it difficult to be compassionate? Explain.

For the "Enemies: Ya Gotta Love 'Em" activity, copy these lists of discussion questions onto pieces of newsprint and tape them to a wall:

(First list)

- When have you realized that someone, for no good reason, just didn't like you?
- How did that feel?
- How did you treat that person?
- Was there something you could have done about the situation?

(Second list)

- How does Jesus say to treat enemies?
- How could you apply Jesus' words to the situations you've described?
- If you rated yourself on how you love your enemies (10 being perfect and 1 being not at all), how would you rate? Explain.
- If you were to pray for your enemies, what would you pray?

(Third list)

- When have you had an enemy—at least for a while—because of something you did?
- How did that feel?
- How did that person treat you?
- How did you treat that person?
- Was there something you could have done to help the situation?

(Fourth list)

- How could you apply Jesus' words to the situation you've described?
- What's the connection between your relationship with God and your relationship with your enemies?
- What can you do if your enemy doesn't show you compassion by reconciling with you?

If you use the Bonus Activity, make a copy of the "Someone's Gotta Pay!" handout (p. 35).

Warm-Up

Compassion Rations
(15 to 20 minutes)

As teenagers arrive, ask them to form groups of three. Have each group use the newspapers and magazines to find a story about enemies. For example, they might find a story about armies attacking each other, a woman battered by her estranged husband, or politicians trashing each other while running for office. Ask each group to be ready to present a report that includes answers to these questions, which you wrote on newsprint before the study:

- **Who are the enemies in your story?**
- **Why are the enemies at odds?**
- **What would it take for the enemies to become friends?**

Allow students to work for five minutes then give their reports. After the reports,

SAY:

- **There's no shortage of enemies in the world. Every one of us has at least one enemy—someone who treats us poorly or looks down on us. Usually our first inclination is to give our enemies the same grief they give us, but that's not how Jesus wants us to respond to enemies. He wants us to choose to love them.**

Read Luke 6:27-36 aloud. Ask groups to discuss these questions, which you wrote on newsprint and posted on the wall before the study:

- **If you were one of the enemies in your story, could you choose to love as Jesus commands? Why or why not?**
- **If the enemies in your story were loving to each other, how would they behave?**
- **Describe a time when you've been compassionate toward someone who treated you poorly. Was it difficult to be compassionate? Explain.**

When groups have finished, have students report again, giving suggestions on how the enemies could be loving to each other. Give volunteers an opportunity to share their answers to the last question. This will help teenagers see ways they can respond in love to situations today.

SAY:

The Point ▶

- **It's easy to find examples of how enemies treat each other, but it can be hard to find examples of people choosing to do what Jesus said to do: Love your enemies. <u>You can *choose* to love everyone, even your enemies.</u> Let's find out more about what Jesus has commanded us to do.**

Enemies: Ya Gotta Love 'Em

(15 to 20 minutes)

Discuss with teenagers various types of enemies. You might talk about how some enemies are "situation" enemies. For instance, if one country declares war on another country, the soldiers of each nation automatically become enemies. It's nothing personal, but they're still shooting at each other.

Other enemies are "personal" enemies—people who dislike us personally. Maybe they don't like our ethnic background, the way we talk, or where we're from. Maybe they dislike our Christian faith.

It's also important to acknowledge to teenagers that it's possible to have an enemy even though we've done nothing to hurt the other person.

Have teenagers form pairs and discuss these questions, which you wrote on newsprint before the study, with their partners:

- **When have you realized that someone, for no good reason, just didn't like you?**
- **How did that feel?**
- **How did you treat that person?**
- **Was there something you could have done about the situation?**

Ask partners to read aloud Matthew 5:43-48 and discuss these questions, which you wrote on newsprint before the study:

- **How does Jesus say to treat enemies?**
- **How could you apply Jesus' words to the situations you've described?**
- **If you rated yourself on how you love your enemies (10 being perfect and 1 being not at all), how would you rate? Explain.**
- **If you were to pray for your enemies, what would you pray?**

When pairs have discussed the questions,

SAY:

- **Sometimes a person may become your enemy because of something you've done. Maybe you accidentally put a rock through someone's window, maybe you gossiped about someone, or maybe you lost someone's autographed Tiger Woods golf shirt. You messed up, and someone dislikes you for it. Maybe that person is even trying to harm you.**

Instruct students to find new partners and discuss these questions, which you wrote on newsprint before the study:

- **When have you had an enemy—at least for a while—because of something you did?**
- **How did that feel?**
- **How did that person treat you?**

- How did you treat that person?
- Was there something you could have done to help the situation?

Ask partners to read aloud Matthew 5:23-24 and discuss these questions, which you wrote on newsprint before the study:

- How could you apply Jesus' words to the situation you've described?
- What's the connection between your relationship with God and your relationship with your enemies?
- What can you do if your enemy doesn't show you compassion by reconciling with you?

Gather the entire group together again and

SAY:

- Jesus made it clear that we're responsible for how we treat our enemies. It's our job to show them compassion and love—no matter how they treat us.

Explain that this means treating our enemies with warmth, respect, and empathy—in other words, we're to see things from their perspective as well as our own. Discuss ways teenagers can share their resources of time, energy, and material to look out for their enemies' best interests.

ASK:

- What are practical ways you can show love and compassion to your enemies?
- Think specifically about a person who has treated you poorly. Without naming names, what does that person need in his or her life? How can you provide it?
- Does Jesus' command to love your enemies make sense to you? Why or why not?

The Point ▶ - What are some ways <u>you can show love to everyone, even your enemies</u>?

✳ Bonus Activity ✳

(15 to 20 minutes)

If you'd like, play this game after the Bible Connection activity. Have teenagers form groups of three or four.

SAY:

- Now we're going to play "Someone's Gotta Pay!"–an exciting new game show that lets contestants be judge and jury in choosing how much to award a person who has been wronged.

Give each team paper and a marker.

 You may want to arrange to have someone videotape this activity. It's not necessary for the completion of the study, but it can add to the fun.

SAY:

■ I'll describe several situations and ask you a question about each one. After I ask you the question, you'll have one minute to come to a decision as a team and write your answer on the paper I've given you.

Read aloud the "Round 1" section from the "Someone's Gotta Pay!" handout (p. 35). Then give teams sixty seconds to write answers.

After one minute, ask teams to display their papers. Award five hundred points to the team whose amount is closest to the true amount.

Continue to read the situations described on the "Someone's Gotta Pay!" handout. For each round, award five hundred points to the team whose guess is closest to the actual amount. In rounds 4 and 5, require teams to explain and justify their answers. Award the points to the team that guesses the highest number or the greatest sacrifice.

After round 5, award bonus points for qualifications such as style, good sportsmanship, and best-tied shoelaces to every team except the team in the lead. Add enough points to each team's score so that each team ends up with the exact same amount of points—making everyone a winner!

When the game is over,

Use these prices as benchmarks to determine which team is closest to an accurate price: The bike costs $1,204; the computer costs $3,294; the dental work costs $2,600.

ASK:

■ What was easy about playing this game? What was difficult?

■ What was it like to put a price on people's suffering?

■ What was it like to compete with another team?

■ How was that similar to having an enemy? How was it different?

■ How did you feel at the end of the game when each team had the same number of points and everybody won? Why?

■ How was that similar to having compassion for an enemy? How was it different?

SAY:

■ Our society believes that people should pay for mistakes. We're quick to place blame and demand payment or revenge when we've been wronged.

Yet no amount of money could really pay for six months of torture. And how could we repay Jesus for what he gave us on the cross? There isn't anything we can do to square the debt we owe. Forgiveness costs us something. When we have compassion for our enemies and show them love by forgiving them, we must let go of our rights to demand revenge. We do for our enemies what Jesus has done for us.

Read Luke 6:27-36 aloud and

ASK:

■ How is what Jesus asks us to do for our enemies like what he did for his enemies? How is it different?

■ What will it cost to treat enemies the way Jesus wants?

■ What's the benefit of treating our enemies this way?

■ Jesus showed his love and compassion for his enemies by dying for us. How can you specifically choose to show love to your enemies? ◄ **The Point**

If you hear howls of protest from the game's "winners" about the "losers" being given an equal reward, consider pausing to investigate Jesus' parable in Matthew 20:1-16.

SAY:

■ When someone commits a wrong, that person owes a debt. When you act with compassion by forgiving an enemy, you love your enemies.

Life Application

Loving and Letting Go
(15 to 20 minutes)

Ask individuals, pairs, or small groups of teenagers to think of several real situations they've faced at the hands of people who treated them as enemies and write them on separate slips of paper. Caution them not to write anything confidential because their slips will be read by others in the group.

Pass a hat and have teenagers put all the slips into the hat. Mix them up, then pass the hat and ask each student to draw out one slip. Have teenagers take turns reading aloud what's written on the slip they chose. Then lead them in brainstorming ways a person could choose to respond in that situation that would be in line with Jesus' command to love our enemies.

Give groups five to ten minutes to discuss their situations, then gather everyone back together.

Give each teenager a very small pebble and a fist-sized stone. Ask teenagers to stand in a circle and face toward the center of the circle, holding their stones or bricks and their pebbles. Place buckets or a tarp (to protect the floor) in the center of the circle.

SAY:

■ **In biblical times, one way people punished enemies and criminals was by crushing their skulls and bones by throwing stones at them. I confess that there have been times when I have chosen not to love my enemies, sometimes for reasons that seem trivial to me now.**

I suspect we've all felt tremendous anger toward an enemy. Maybe you're feeling it now. Take a moment to think of someone you would define as an enemy in your life.

Pause for several seconds, then encourage teenagers to let go of their anger so they can act with compassion toward their enemies. Perhaps they need to forgive an enemy, do what's best for an enemy, try to see things from their enemy's point of view, or begin to treat an enemy with respect.

Explain that when you give the cue, "Because of what Jesus has done for me, I will love my enemy," you'll move to the center of the circle and release your stone as you release your anger. Encourage students who are willing to release their anger toward an enemy and give up their desire to hurt an enemy to repeat the words after you and do as you do. Let teenagers know that if they don't feel comfortable with this commitment, it's OK to just spend the time praying, asking God to help them come to the point where they can love their enemies.

Walk to the middle of the circle as you

SAY:

■ **Because of what Jesus has done for me, I will love my enemy.**

Your teenagers may have good reasons to be angry. Maybe they're being abused, or perhaps they're suffering in another ongoing, unjust situation. Don't demand that they release their stones. Be sure to affirm teenagers even if they don't. But also be sure to follow up and provide a listening ear. Your teenagers need to know that you care about what they're going through. Help them resolve their situations, or refer them to someone who can.

Then drop your stone into a bucket or onto the tarp.

When everyone who wants to has had a chance to repeat after you, pray aloud. Thank God for the courage of the teenagers who released their anger and for the honesty of the teenagers who didn't release their stones. Ask God to show teenagers how to move toward lives of compassion and love for their enemies. Pray that God will help them to <u>choose to show love to everyone,</u>   ◀ **The Point** <u>even their enemies</u>. Thank God for the example set by Jesus.

After your prayer, instruct any students still holding their pebbles to place the pebbles in their shoes and leave them there until they've shown love to an enemy—or until they've taken a step toward letting go of their anger and loving an enemy. This pebble can be a reminder that they've been forgiven so much by Jesus, and that they can share a tiny bit of compassion with another person.

SOMEONE'S *Gotta Pay!*

Round 1

A careless driver spilled coffee on his lap while he was cruising through a neighborhood. His car jumped over the curb and [cr]ushed the new dual-suspension, specialized, twenty-[fo]ur-speed mountain bike Dana had left parked outside [th]e Yummy-Freeze. Someone's gotta pay! What will it [co]st the driver to replace Dana's bike?

Round 2

While he was jostling with his buddy for control of the school's new laptop with the 1 GHz G4 processor, 17-inch display, and [Su]perDrive DVD-R/CDRW, Eddie Goldfarb yanked hard, [se]nding the computer flying out a third-floor window. [W]hen it hit the sidewalk, there wasn't enough computer [le]ft to solder together a calculator. Someone's gotta [pa]y! What will it cost Eddie to replace the laptop?

Round 3

Sheila knew she shouldn't sneak up and fire a snowball at the back of Jeff's head...but she did. Jeff turned at exactly the wrong [m]oment, and the snowball knocked out his two front [te]eth. Now Jeff needs a dental bridge. Someone's gotta [pa]y! How much money should Sheila give Jeff?

Round 4

When Denise moved to Malvia, she felt safe...until the government toppled and she was taken hostage. She was imprisoned and tortured for nearly six months, then suddenly released when Malvia's military dictator was overthrown. Her former captors are now coming to trial. Someone's gotta pay! How should they repay Denise for her experience?

Round 5

God sent his only Son to earth to live with us—the King of the universe living with people who didn't deserve help. In fact, we were sinners and had made ourselves enemies of God by rejecting him and turning away from him. Jesus provided an example of how to treat enemies by letting us kill him—by willingly dying in our place—to pay the price of our sin. Someone's gotta pay! What price should we pay God for what we put Jesus through?

Seeking the Holy Spirit's Guidance

guidance

HOLY SPIRIT

"**I** was leaning against the gym wall when Bill ran past me. I don't know why, but I tripped him. I didn't have a grudge against Bill. I wasn't trying to show off for my friends. I put my foot out 'just because.' Maybe I wanted to see what would happen or if I could time it just right. I did.

"At first, I was delighted. Then Bill grabbed his elbow and looked up at me. He didn't say a word. I immediately felt regret. I couldn't understand why I did it. I guess I acted on impulse, and Bill fell to the ground."

How many harmful choices could we avoid if we took the time to seek the Holy Spirit's direction before we act? How much pain could we avoid if we always, even for a millisecond, stopped and asked, "Should I do this, God?" before rushing ahead. Contrary to common belief, self-control isn't mastery over carnal lust. It's submission to God's will. We exercise self-control when we delay our immediate impulses in order to ask the Holy Spirit for guidance in the choices we make. This study will show teenagers how to rely on God's guidance as they seek to honor him in their daily lives.

The Study at a Glance

Warm-Up (15-20 minutes)

The Hearing Heard
What students will do: Play a game of blindfolded Tag and compare the game with seeking the Holy Spirit's guidance.

Needs:
- ❏ Bibles
- ❏ 2 baseball caps
- ❏ paper
- ❏ "Rules for Big Trouble in Little Quad-Wrangle" handouts (p. 44)
- ❏ blindfolds
- ❏ masking tape
- ❏ markers

Bonus Activity (10-15 minutes)

What students will do: Play Who Wants to Make the Right Choices? and learn that the Holy Spirit is always available as the "expert" to help them make right choices.

Needs:
- ❏ paper
- ❏ pens

Bible Connection (20-25 minutes)

Creative Difference
What students will do: Examine the poor choices made by some biblical characters and decide how following the Holy Spirit's direction would have changed the outcomes.

Needs:
- ❏ Bibles
- ❏ pens
- ❏ markers
- ❏ newsprint
- ❏ tape
- ❏ "Whoops!" handouts (p. 45)

Life Application (10-15 minutes)

Lifeline
What students will do: Examine personal choices and make a choice to follow the Holy Spirit's guidance in the future.

Needs:
- ❏ "Lifeline" handouts (p. 46)
- ❏ markers
- ❏ string

The Point

We should rely on God's Spirit to help us make good choices.

Scripture Source

Judges 15:9-16; 16:15-30; 1 Samuel 16:11-19; 2 Samuel 11:1-5; 12:7-14, 19-24; Matthew 16:13-19; Mark 14:66-72; John 21:15-19

These passages tell stories of men who were called by God, made poor choices, faced the consequences of their choices, and were restored by God.

Psalms 32:8-9; 48:14

These psalms explain that God guides his people.

John 16:7-8

Jesus promises the coming of the Holy Spirit.

guidance

HOLY SPIRIT

For "The Hearing Heard" activity, use masking tape to create a giant square on the floor of your meeting room. Write "Big Trouble" on a piece of paper, and tape it to the front of a baseball cap. Write "Impulse" on another piece of paper, and tape it to a different baseball cap. Make a copy of the "Rules for Big Trouble in Little Quad-Wrangle" handout (p. 44) for every two students.

If you use the Bonus Activity, write the answer to each question from the Who Wants to Make the Right Choices? quiz (p. 40) on a separate slip of paper.

For the "Creative Difference" activity, make one copy of the "Whoops!" handout (p. 45) for each student. Also, write the following instructions on a sheet of newsprint:

How would your character's life have been different if he had stopped and asked the Holy Spirit for direction before he chose to sin? Demonstrate your answer by choosing one of the following options:

1. Present a mini-musical of the character's story.

2. Rewrite the character's story, setting it in modern times. Then read it to the class.

3. Present an interview with the character.

4. Draw a scene from the life of the character.

5. Create a mathematical equation that describes the character's choices and the consequences of those decisions.

Tape the instructions to a wall, and set markers and sheets of newsprint on the floor near it.

For the "Lifeline" activity, make a copy of the "Lifeline" handout (p. 46) for each student. Cut a piece of string, approximately three inches long, for each student.

The Hearing Heard
(15 to 20 minutes)

As teenagers arrive, have them form pairs. Give each pair a blindfold and a copy of the "Rules for Big Trouble in Little Quad-Wrangle" handout (p. 44). Give one pair both of the baseball caps. Then read the rules aloud as teenagers follow along. When everyone understands the game, tell the Seekers and Big Trouble to put on their blindfolds. Have teenagers play the game for five minutes, then prompt partners to switch places and play the game again. After another five minutes, end the game and ask teenagers to form groups of four and discuss these questions:

■ What was the hardest part about guiding the Seeker?
■ What was the hardest part about following the Guide?

Short on blindfolds? Consider using clean socks, shirts, towels, handkerchiefs, or rags. Tie pieces of the material together so the blindfolds are large enough to fit around the students' heads.

Invite two students to read aloud John 16:7-8 and Psalm 48:14, then

ASK:

■ How is the Holy Spirit like the Guide? Share examples from your everyday life.
■ How are you like the Seeker? Explain.
■ What's the hardest part about following the Holy Spirit's guidance?

Call the groups back together and ask a volunteer to read Psalm 32:8-9 aloud. Then

SAY:

■ <u>We can rely on God's Spirit to help us make good</u> ◄ **The Point**
<u>choices in life.</u> Sometimes we don't make the best choices because we don't seek his direction before we act. While we have the freedom to make our own decisions, the Holy Spirit wants us to make choices that bring us closer to him. That's why it's so important to seek his guidance before we make decisions.

Be careful not to give the baseball caps to a pair of teenagers in which one or both of them may struggle with his or her physical appearance or self-image. Directly asking a student to play the part labeled "Big Trouble" may inadvertently cause him or her to feel belittled.

Don't worry if students must play the part of Big Trouble more than once. A random label is perceived in a much different light than a direct role assignment from the leader.

Some of the teenagers in your group may not have a foundational understanding of the Holy Spirit's identity. If this is true, direct them to John 14:15-21; 16:7-15; and 1 Corinthians 2:10-12. Have a volunteer read each passage aloud. After each passage has been read, ask the group what the verses say about who the Holy Spirit is.

(10 to 15 minutes)

If you have time, play Who Wants to Make the Right Choices? after "The Hearing Heard" activity.

Give each teenager a pen and a piece of paper, and ask them to number from one to ten down the left-hand side. Distribute slips of paper, with the answer to one of the quiz questions on each slip. If you have fewer than ten students, give more than one to some or all, or keep some for yourself.

SAY:

■ I'm going to read you a series of multiple-choice questions. Your job is to choose which answer is the right one. If you're pretty sure you know the answer on your own, great. Mark it down.

Keep track of any questions you're not sure about. When we're finished, you can ask someone else for help. The answer to each question has been distributed to an "expert" in our class. You must choose which person you believe has the correct answer to the question you're debating and ask him or her for help.

The rules are simple. You can only ask one person for his or her expert advice on your question. If someone asks you for the answer to the question for which you've been given the "expert" answer, you must tell that person the truth. If, however, you did not receive that answer, you can't reveal that fact. You can answer the question to the best of your ability, or you can try to deliberately lead them astray.

When all the students understand the rules, read the following questions and possible answers:

1. How many colors are in a rainbow?
   a. 7
   b 11
   c. 14
   d. 28

2. What's the largest American state (in land mass)?
   a. Alaska
   b. Texas
   c. California
   d. Montana

3. What's the world's largest sea?
   a. the Red
   b. the Sea of Tranquility
   c. the Mediterranean
   d. the Baltic

4. What is the capital of Missouri?
   a. St. Louis
   b. Kansas City
   c. Jefferson City
   d. Joplin

5. What is the chemical symbol for iron?
   a. Ne
   b. I
   c. Ir
   d. Fe

6. At what speed does sound travel?
   a. 500 mph
   b. 700 mph
   c. 5,000 mph
   d. 70,000 mph

7. What was the last state admitted to the United States?
   a. Alaska
   b. Hawaii
   c. New Mexico
   d. Puerto Rico

8. When did the Korean War start?
   a. 1940
   b. 1950
   c. 1964
   d. 1991

How far is the longest recorded distance traveled by a bird?

    a. about 160 miles

    b. about 1,600 miles

    c. about 16,000 miles

    d. about 160,000 miles

10. How many major blood types are there?

    a. 2

    b. 4

    c. 5

    d. 10

Answer Key: 1. a, **7—**red, orange, yellow, green, blue, indigo, and violet; **2.** a, Alaska; **3.** c, the Mediterranean; **4.** c, Jefferson City; **5.** d, Fe; **6.** b, 700 mph; **7.** b, Hawaii; **8.** b, 1950; **9.** c, about 16,000 miles; **10.** b, 4—A, B, AB, and O.

When everyone has finished seeking help on difficult questions, give students one more minute to finalize their answers. Then share the correct answers.

ASK:

- ■ Did asking the "experts" for help make getting the right answers easier or more difficult? Why?
- ■ The right answers were all there. What made it so difficult for you to find them?
- ■ What would have made it easier?
- ■ How is this like trying to make good decisions in life?

SAY:

- ■ We should rely on the Holy Spirit to help us make good choices. He wants us to ask for his help. He always knows the right thing to do, and he is eager to help us. He can always be our lifeline. No matter how many times a day we need his help, he's always able and willing.

◄ **The Point**

Bible Connection

Creative Difference

(20 to 25 minutes)

Distribute the "Whoops!" handout (p. 45). Have teenagers form three groups. Assign one of the following characters to each group: Samson, Peter, and David. Ask each group to discuss the questions found under the name of its character.

When the teenagers finish,

SAY:

- ■ How would your Bible character's life have been different if he'd stopped and asked the Holy Spirit for direction before choosing to sin? Give a short explanation of the biblical story to the class. Then show the difference that following the Holy Spirit's direction would have made by choosing one of the five options from the list on the wall. For example, if your character is Samson, you can explain his encounter with Delilah and then present a mini-musical that shows

If you have more than fifteen teenagers in your group, have them form groups of four. Assign each Bible character to more than one group as needed.

how Samson's life would have been different if he'd sought the Holy Spirit's direction before choosing to reveal his secret.

Encourage teenagers to use the newsprint and markers you set out before the study to help them brainstorm and prepare their presentations. Give the groups about ten to fifteen minutes to prepare and make their presentations.

SAY:

■ All three of these Bible characters acted without much self-control. All three of them paid a price for their reckless choices. We've learned from these stories that we should rely on God's Spirit to help us make good choices. We need to stop before we act, even if it's just for a split second, and ask him to guide us in the choices we make.

◄ **The Point**

Lifeline
(10 to 15 minutes)

Life Application

Gather teenagers together, and give each student a copy of the "Lifeline" handout (p. 46). Place markers in the center of the group.

SAY:

■ I'd like you to evaluate every year of your life since first grade. If you think first grade was a good year, put a dot in the first grade column that corresponds with the rating. If it was the best year of your life, put the dot near ten. If it was the worst year, put the dot near zero. Write one word above or below the dot that explains why it was a good or bad year. Do this for every grade on the sheet. When you get to a number that's higher than the grade you're currently in, put the dot in a place that shows how you think that year will be for you.

Give teenagers about five minutes to make their lifelines. Then have students form pairs. Ask them to circle the two best grades and the two worst grades of their lives. Have the pairs discuss the following questions:

■ Are the grades you circled good or bad because of choices you made, choices others made, or things that happened to you? Explain.
■ Look at the two lowest grades. If everyone involved in the situations had stopped and sought the Holy Spirit's direction before acting, would the situations have been different? If so, how?

Ask pairs to tell the God-honoring characteristics they see in each other that may make the future better than the past has been. Ask teenagers to decide how they're going to follow the Holy Spirit's guidance in the future, and have them tell their partners what they've resolved to do. Then

SAY:

The Point ▶

■ Seeking the Holy Spirit's direction won't make our lives perfect. We can't control everything that happens to us. We can, however, choose to seek the Holy Spirit's guidance on how to react to those situations. <u>We should rely on the Holy Spirit to help us make good choices.</u> Following the Holy Spirit's direction won't give us a pain-free life, but it will help us avoid sin and unnecessary suffering.

To close, ask students to spend a few minutes thinking about choices they're facing in the coming week: how they'll act toward the kid who's picked on at school, how they'll respond when their parents tell them to do or not to do something, how they'll prioritize their lives, and so on. Encourage them to spend a few minutes in prayer, asking the Holy Spirit to guide them and give them wisdom to make God-honoring choices. Give each student a short piece of string, and have teenagers tie a bow around one of their partner's fingers as a reminder to ask the Holy Spirit for help whenever they are choosing how to act.

To gauge how your students have been applying these studies on *Choosing Wisely* to their everyday lives, consider using the Changed 4 Life idea found on page 47. To implement this Changed 4 Life strategy, you'll need to set aside a few minutes at the end of this last Bible study, so make sure to plan ahead.

Rules for Big Trouble in Little Quad-Wrangle

1. All players must stay within the tape outline. If you go outside of the boundaries, you and your partner must sit out of the game for thirty seconds.

2. If you don't have a cap, choose one person in your pair to be the Seeker. The other person is the Guide.

3. If you have a cap, choose one person to be Big Trouble. The other person is Impulse. Put on the cap that matches your role.

4. Big Trouble and the Seekers must wear blindfolds.

5. The Seekers and Big Trouble must walk by placing one foot directly in front of the other, heel to toe, as if they were walking on a tightrope.

6. Big Trouble must try to tag the Seekers.

7. Guides must direct their Seekers away from Big Trouble by using only verbal commands.

8. Impulse must guide Big Trouble to the Seekers by using only verbal commands.

9. Impulse and the Guides may not touch anyone.

10. If Big Trouble tags a Seeker, the Seeker becomes Big Trouble and must wear the Big Trouble cap. That person's Guide then becomes Impulse and must wear the Impulse cap. The players formerly known as Big Trouble and Impulse take the roles of Seeker and Guide, respectively.

SAMSON

Read Judges 15:9-16.

Why did the Israelites hand over their own warrior to the Philistines?

What was the result of their choice to hand him over?

Where did Samson find his strength?

Was God with Samson? Explain.

Read Judges 16:15-22.

Why do you think Samson told Delilah the secret of his strength?

What was the result of his choice?

Read Judges 16:23-30.

How was Samson's attitude different from before?

What choice did Samson make?

What was the result of this choice?

PETER

READ MATTHEW 16:13-19.

What was Jesus' opinion of Peter?

Why do you think Jesus felt this way about Peter?

READ MARK 14:66-72.

Why do you think Peter denied Jesus?

Do you think this choice changed Jesus' opinion of Peter? If so, how?

Did the choice change Peter's opinion of himself? If so, how?

READ JOHN 21:15-19.

What did Jesus ask of Peter? Why?

Did Jesus' attitude toward Peter change? If so, how?

DAVID

Read 1 Samuel 16:11-19.

Why did God choose David to be anointed as king?

Read 2 Samuel 11:1-5; 12:7-14.

Why did David make the choice to commit adultery?

What was the result of this choice?

What was David's reaction to Nathan's accusation?

What was the result of David's choice to confess his sin?

Read 2 Samuel 12:19-24.

How did God feel about David after he committed adultery?

Did God restore David? If so, how?

OK2COPY

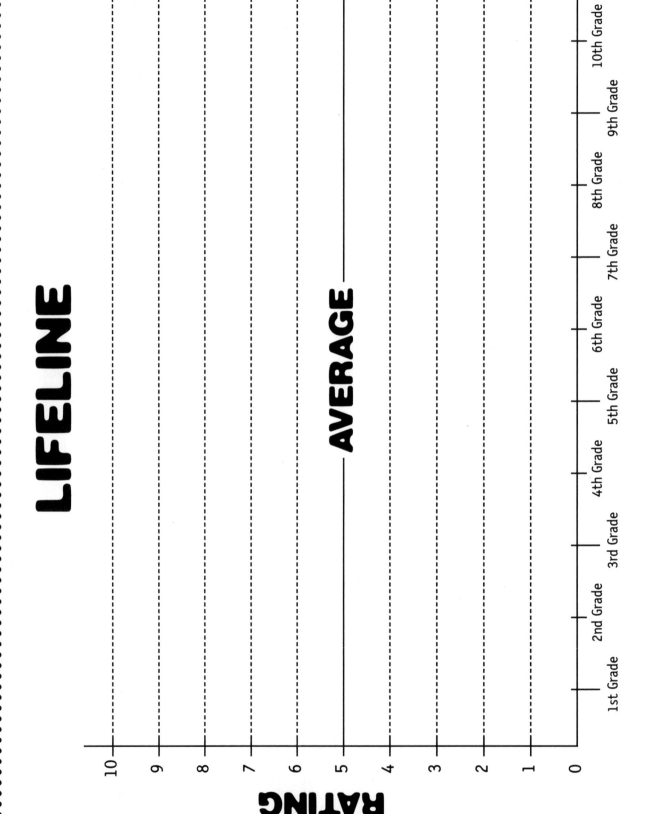

LIFELINE

AVERAGE

1st Grade 2nd Grade 3rd Grade 4th Grade 5th Grade 6th Grade 7th Grade 8th Grade 9th Grade 10th Grade

RATING

10
9
8
7
6
5
4
3
2
1
0